New Moon Montage

By CD Harvey

Table of Contents

New Moon Montage

Again darkness prevails

Gone is light

Shone in other evenings

Cycles begin

Peace transcends all

The moon will rise again

Trees sing vespers

Leaves turn and die in full regalia

Warmth forsaken

Undermined by crisp autumn nights

The haughtiness of summer

Given endless change

Buffalo bones dance with

Grandfather and i

Ushering in the new moon

On these nights

Whispers echoing above the fire recall

Dying

Open eyes embracing darkness

Birthing

An infant nursing in the predawn light

And through it all we move within circles

Timeless

Yet closing quickly

Why am I here

I stare into the night

Stars fill. The sky

I search for a clue

Why am I here?

The stars not confused by this divine comedy

Laugh as if to say

That they are immortal

And I!

I am just meteor falling from the sky

On the Savannah

As I am

I shall remain

Billowing wind of springtime fame

Bringing rainclouds

Drummers of a billion

Pound the beat

The universal tune

I sweep and swirl

Every hill a sacred shrine

The earth is soil

All is mine

I am endless

We all breathe together

To a leaf

To a feather

On the savannah

This small world

Into the hinterland

Towards hamlets of folklore

Rivers without bridges

Forests primeval left unfelt

Wisemen born of nature

Midwives bred with herbs

Fluid graceful forms

Edify the greatness

Of this small world

Heavenly father

Knows mother god well

Our practice of fertility

Serves his purpose

If we do it right

Crops will grow to completion

And at the end

The sickle strikes quick

Laying the wheat low

Their death provides life

When the earth grows hard and barren

In the springtime of the gods

Everything was possible

We danced to Astarte

And our crops grew well

We drank ceremonial wine

Bowing to tribal gods

The world was small

With dragons on the corners

Memory

Voices whisper from ages past

Revealing their mysteries

Tribes turn to nations

Nations to sand

Testing every deviation

Memory never forgets

Too stubborn to change coarse

Remembering the rule

Dust to dust

Death of a God

Me thought me immortal

Never a dying day

The universe to roam

With jokes to play

Dominion had I

Over creatures everywhere

Mortals would seek me

Through prayer

As their knowledge grew

They did shun

Their own divinity to prove

Misguided daughters and suns

They took from me the breath

All living things need

Confined me to a book

Which only scholars read

Fear

Fear still haunts me

A distorted dream

Springing from purgatory

"clinging desperately to"

A forgotten memory

Perhaps from childhood

Near erased in gleeful moments

Fear emanates from

Evenings dark

Dark memories

And the uncharted areas

Of my brain

Feigning Disdain

Tucked away beneath disdain

Humor

Hiding from curious sight

Trying to remain aloof

In spite of sacred night

Night sacred

An amorous ray of light

Reflects off the windowpane

And casually sifts away

Moths

I will not be deluded

From my frithing froth

Glorious incantations of boring moths

I stare incessantly at a bright light

Watching circumnavigation

Carried out by night

Binging

Banging

Against the shinning bulb

Fluttering

Failing

Living mindlessly

Till falling from sight

I flick the switch

Goodnight

An Effort to Converse

I set my feet to walking

The sun breaks across the plain

My soul commences talking

To my mistress once again

I set my heart to singing

A song of familiar verse

It seems the winds enjoying

My effort to converse

The sun is its place now

Showering the earth with light

My countenance is content

Just to watch the birds in flight

Warm Breeze

A warm breeze

Heats the soil of the earth

Flows so delicately all around

Tickles your skin

Caresses your hair

And soon you are forsaken

For it has left you

Standing there

A Flowers Fable

Seed of finest flower

Was planted in his garden

Springing to sprout

Not being forgotten

Sun showered solar rays

Rain fell on this flower

Growing to maturity

A proud summer tower'

At last the gardener sheared

To rest upon the table

Petals drop as tears

Ending this fable

Generations of Lazarus

Amongst human wastelands

Generations of Lazarus

Clinging to sand

Life a fragile trust

Blisters on infirm bodies

Outwardly signify strife

Distressing to any creed

Hiding from blight

(The rich man's riddle)

They should be swept from the street

Then our cities would be neat

We pay taxes for good government

Our sidewalks garbage dumps

The rich man doesn't remember

He thinks himself divine

But at conclusion loses nerve

His name in scripture

He cannot find

2000lbs. of Squid

Look

Look at me

Try hard

It isn't me

Laugh

She did

Two 2000lbs of squid

You're joking

My belly stroking

I will go no more a roaming

Fickle fortune far too shallow

Joke I tried

I tried

The trees knew

The roses lied

Driving in my car

Gas can take me

Just so far

This is useless

Just say when

Fickle fortune far too shallow

Final

The end

No more letters to send

Obvious I should have known

All care

To the wind blown

Calm no choice

My eyes moist

Fickle fortune

Far too shallow

Fair Maiden 2

She was a captive exile

Hidden in her beliefs

The smallest of transgressions

Made her feel like a thief

She was a fine dancer

Although she danced alone

Away from the judges

Who would only cast stones

She sang in the choir

High up in the loft

Her thoughts true devotion

And the price that it cost

She never knew autumn

Which comes after the fall

Or the sinful world around her

She had her call

Poor damn Icarus

Icarus flew a bit too high

Wax dripping from his wings

Plunging

Finally

The ultimate cost

Flying wasn't what he'd dreamed

Old Emily

She brought us laughter when there was rain

A small intense woman of storytelling fame

Her voice was low a thunder

And she used it well

To conjure up images in which children could dwell

She blew smoke clouds that danced above her head

Her eyes telling all that she had not said

She has long since gone to heaven

For another show

The angels must be smiling

As they polish their halos

Fair Maiden

There once was a fair maiden

Who adored friendly faces

Fresh air

She had a gift so beautiful

All would stare

She danced in April rain

December snow

Time went on

Causing change

Losing recollection of her past

Her former self waned

She dreamed of April rain

December snow

She was caught desire

Pursued by her lusts

A forgone conclusion

Her innocence dust

There were no rains in April

Or December snows

Then a robin sang a melody

From swaddled nest

Bringing a longing within her breast

For rains in April

And December snows

Pax Romana

I was spent

That night by her side

Halfway between reality and nirvana

Frost on windowpane by the bed in which we lay

She spoke of love abounding

As I listened to the pounding of her heart

Love for feathered touch

My way of saying her name

She asked me if ii loved her

I said I didn't know

But in my heart

I knew

I was conquered

Thoughts of a withering leaf

The musty smell of harvest

Happy children laughing

Have gone home to mother

It's warmer there

Babel

What came down from the tower

Wasn't what had gone up

The end of foolish cooperation

The good lord did disrupt

Notice

Closer than once I'd thought

Resting in plain sight

Taking just a break in time

To end this oversight

Gossip

Tasting the kill

I went for throat

I swallowed the pill

And ate the goat

Ajar

Anxious was I to go away

from what I'd known before

But to my dismay I did not like

What stood behind the door

She Kissed a Frog

She kissed a frog that told her

I am a handsome prince

The frog remained a frog

In a state of bliss

A More Convenient Time

Fortune smiles upon my soul

I look into your eyes

Wonderful thoughts pass through my mind

But finding them too difficult

To define

I painfully wait

For a more convenient time

Wind chime

Separate from the others shaped differently

Perplex when in harmony

Your part to play

Yet it has not been like this forever

Someone has formed you

Placed you on this wall

But when the wind rushes to bring music

You are your all in all

Reflection

A broken mirror tells you are here

To speak about another
'
Who seeks you're affection

With straightened glass

Old fashioned class

Minor imperfections

I Am Awake

A smile is on my lips

My skin grows dark in the sun

I thank the heavens for having led me to this place

I am awake to nature and knowledge

Strength permeates my soul

Confidence in my environment is assured

Environment is controlled by my soul

All is sacred

Midday rain showers

The crying of infants

Everything has its place

Kiva

Darkness prevails

Along the canyon floor

Stars even further

In the new moon sky

My heart full of despair

When I hear the coyote cry

Shaman danced eons before

Sunken temples in the valley

Now highways and mini malls adorn

Hear the Shaman cry

An infant crying in the pre -dawn light

Proof that we 've survived the night

Hope in eyes not dimmed by sin

So we all can begin again

Hear the baby cry

Loft

Rising above

Separation

A brightly colored

Spring bought balloon

Secret

Evening comes to the Nile

This land gives very little away

The exact practices of the temple builders

Sealed forever on the lips

Of a silent sphinx

Eros Venus

My earth ware mother

My springtime bride

Entwined in flowers

Loving again

Sans virginity

Restore our fallen wasteland

Spirits whisper in the valley

Mysteries of life in perfect form

Eroded as the memory of the adult

Recalling infant days

Surely an eagle flew here

Keen eyes surveying all

Surely man perverted Zion

On the way to the promised land

Circle of Seasons

Outside the leaves are changing

Soon earth will be their destination

That's how the circle of seasons goes

They were buds in early spring

Sun and rain helped to make them whole

Their colors paint my avenue

Oh, how well you know me

Words fail to tell my point of view

I can't express my gratitude

In my life leaves are changing

I have no clue of their destination

But their changing just the same

Thank you for walking with me

Down my avenue

Watching the circle of seasons go

Children in Spring

Cries of laughter fill the air

An old man in his chair

Stares in amusement at children playing

A boy is a pilot at war

An ace taking his place among the clouds

Girls dance with ballerina grace

While another

Ties her shoelaces

For as their memory he has been there

The same old man in his chair

One boy makes his way to say hello

"How old are you? the child asks

"As old as time" the man replies

The child smiles unable to comprehend

Then runs off to join children again

To a Friend

Lost in the vestment of your pride

Faith in earthly devotion

Subjective unto to death you carried the day

Oh, what devasted you so

What cross or titan stone

What strange reality within yourself!

Forced denial

The veil that covered one

Why did you reject life?

Suffocating yourself and those of us that loved

Tel

It was alive once

A community at the crossroads

Pot shards remember

Layers of brick upon the sand

This mound

A cycle of civilizations

That arose

Then died

Morning light and Twilight

In dreams I speak to her morning light

A vision of first love and innocent delight

She has her expectations too

For I am twilight

The messenger of night

I know what she doesn't

She has what I have lost

I have done the forbidden

In these blessed moments I speak to her

Of what little time we have

To merge with one another

Magnifying the earth

I gather in morning light

She tucks me away

Twilight

Will O' the Wisp

What's left behind cannot be gathered

Although the moon and stars play tricks

I have seen but could not hold

The will o' the wisp

I've seen a goddess clothed in light

My true desire to be with her there

To possess her till dawn comes stealing

The stars from morning air

What I sought was pristine beauty

That first eternal kiss

But few and far

Are the bogs and woodlands that hold

The will o' the wisp

Daughter of the Stars

Earth is a troublesome place for a daughter of the stars

Set apart before the northeaster blew

That the heavens saw it fit

To bestow a spirit strong within you

Righteousness is hard to find in this land below

But you have the love of all that radiates and glows

Tracing itself back to the stars

And your celestial home

Pure Love

Love is far too difficult to define

Constraint put on this lofty emotion

Is to wrestle the waves in the ocean

Or hold for ransom that which is not mine

Although tempted I choose not to cross that line

In this way I shall prove my devotion

Enslaving love is a silly notion

I breathe and so must cherished love reborn

Taking away what was a bitter sting

To fly again on the nightingale's wing

Bringing cheer to what was so sad and torn

Removing indifference as a thorn

No more will I seek for sorrows to cling

Love unrestrained is a beautiful thing

Sans Virginity

Restore our fallen wilderness

Spirits whisper in the valley

Mysteries of life in perfect form

Eroded as the memory of the adult

Recalling infant days

Surely an eagle flew here

Keen eyes surveying all

Surely man perverted Zion

On his way to the promised land

Kuwait City (From the Water Tower)

Against the minaret I saw

Flames from oil wells burning

100 or so illuminating the night

Beautiful at first thought

This fruit of destruction

An ancient culture

Fratricide

To kill a brother

Patriarchs had wandered near here

Mohammed stirred the sands

Caravans plied their trade

In this cradle of man

And it was clear

The nightingale had left her ancestral home

Consigned forever

To folklore

Shiite Girl

It was hot as always

Straining against the middle eastern sun

We were called to transport directly

The Shiite girl

She in play dress

Her left leg lost to a mine

It wasn't hard to figure what her fate must be

She lives in the third world

Quite apart from the technology we know

I tried not to be moved

Work in a professional way

Watched tears stream across her face

And I began to weep

Moving Day

For us that were assigned ambulances

It is and always moving day

The sadistic sun

Unforgiving

Unrepentant

A silent witness to everything

We

waiting for movement and relief

Then it happens

Come quickly

Action

2 body bags

O.D. green

Accidental death

"Does cause matter?"

A pick -up truck pulled up

The tail gate broken

My partner and I

Hoisted our body bag over the side

The ancient docs dropped theirs

Gasping in shock

The driver was to happy

Paper thin

Ghoulish

Quipped

"He can't feel it anyway"

I lit a smoke

They were young

New to the army

Now on their way

To the refrigeration warehouse

Fanatic

In the hollowness of a hateful heart

Reason is told to get the hell out

No council is thought of and none is given

Outside the inner circle none are forgiven

The chosen speak inciting revolution

Evil reigns free seeking retribution

What they seek indeed they find

Blood is more a liquor than wine

Innocence dies for the greater cause

No price too high to change the laws

An act of war is not a crime

Washed clean with the passage of time

When the smoke clears

From the morning sky

The fanatic cheers and the mourners cry

Icon

Ask me sweetly

Ask me soft

The politician said with a smile

Kill the poet

Pay the scribe

Paradise

The last hungry child was fed

Trumpets filling heaven

At last new Jerusalem

The prophets watched astounded

The Doomed Affair

It happened so quickly

Eyes

Then bodies meeting

Then the mating

Intense but insecure

A dream retold in the council of my thoughts

Blindfolded and spinning

I the Moth

I fly unto yonder light

Throwing caution to the wind

There is blackness in the night

Thoughts of what could have been

These are desperate times

My wings can carry just so much

I do not know what I'll find

I am delicate to the touch

I fly unto yonder light

For what awaits me there

My curiosity will be answered

All else I do not care

Façade

Too shallow is the covering

For it can't hold much weight

To whimsical to stop

The inexorable tide of fate

Conceived in haste or desperation

Poor masonry work compared to woman walls

Nor deep and moving as Solomon's temple halls

Autumn Now

Autumn my sanctuary

This multi -colored abode

Rich with the hues harvest has wrought

Passing quickly

A short- lived affair

Familiar as an old lover

Clouds that once brought rain

Foreshadow coming snow

Made in the USA
Monee, IL
05 August 2021